The RUTH BADER GINSBURG COLORING BOOK

W9-CPB-262

A Tribute to the Always Colorful and Often Inspiring Life of the Supreme Court Justice Known as RBG

TOM F. O'LEARY

ISBN-13: 978-0692644782

ISBN-10: 0692644784

Visit us at www.gumdroppress.com

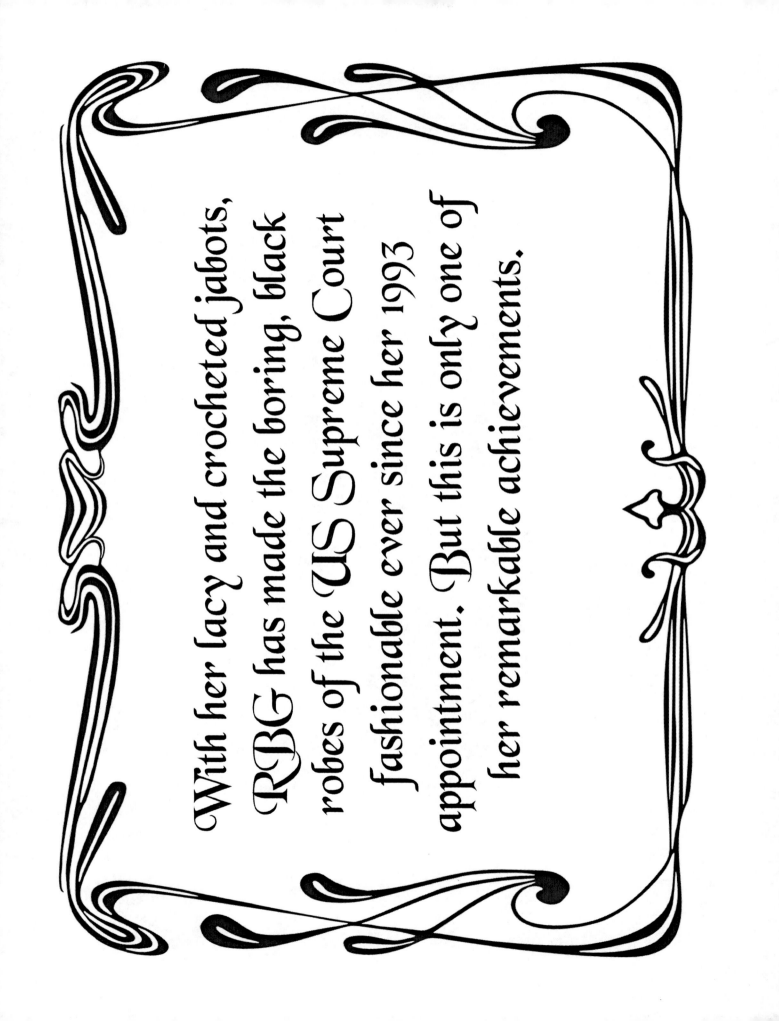

With her lacy and crocheted jabots, RBG has made the boring, black robes of the US Supreme Court fashionable ever since her 1993 appointment. But this is only one of her remarkable achievements.

When President Barack Obama delivered his first speech to Congress in 2009, RBG hugged him, later saying, "There was a rapport from the start between us."

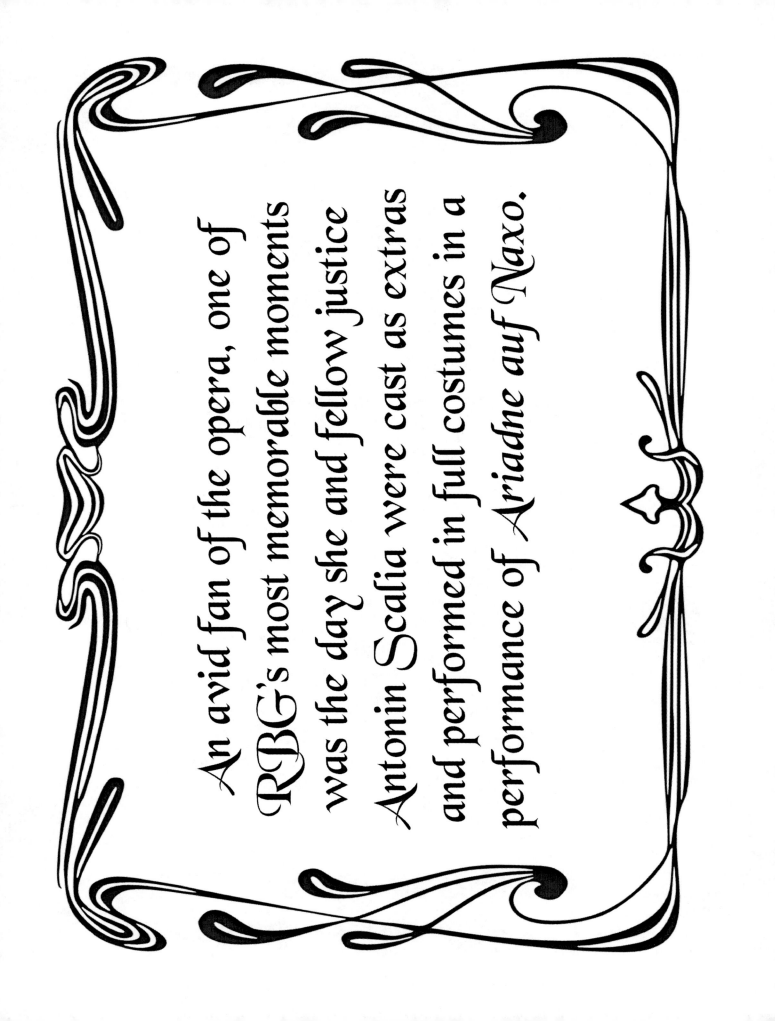

An avid fan of the opera, one of RBG's most memorable moments was the day she and fellow justice Antonin Scalia were cast as extras and performed in full costumes in a performance of Ariadne auf Naxo.

Despite her fondness for Obama, RBG was caught on camera dozing during his 2015 State of the Union address. "I wasn't 100% sober," she admitted, adding that she'd imbibed wine at dinner with some of her fellow justices.

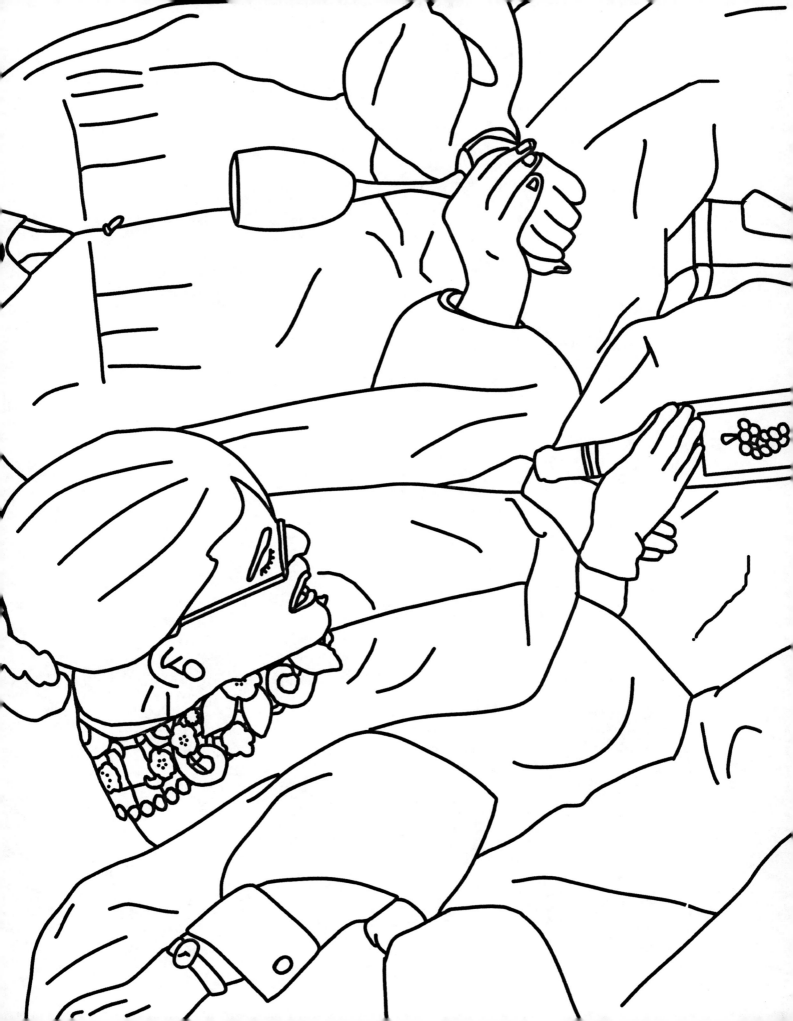

In the 1990s, RBG, like Buffy the Vampire Slayer, was busy putting the "grr" in girl. Her notoriously scorching dissents and outspoken candor were already becoming the stuff of legend, and she never backed down from a fight that mattered to her.

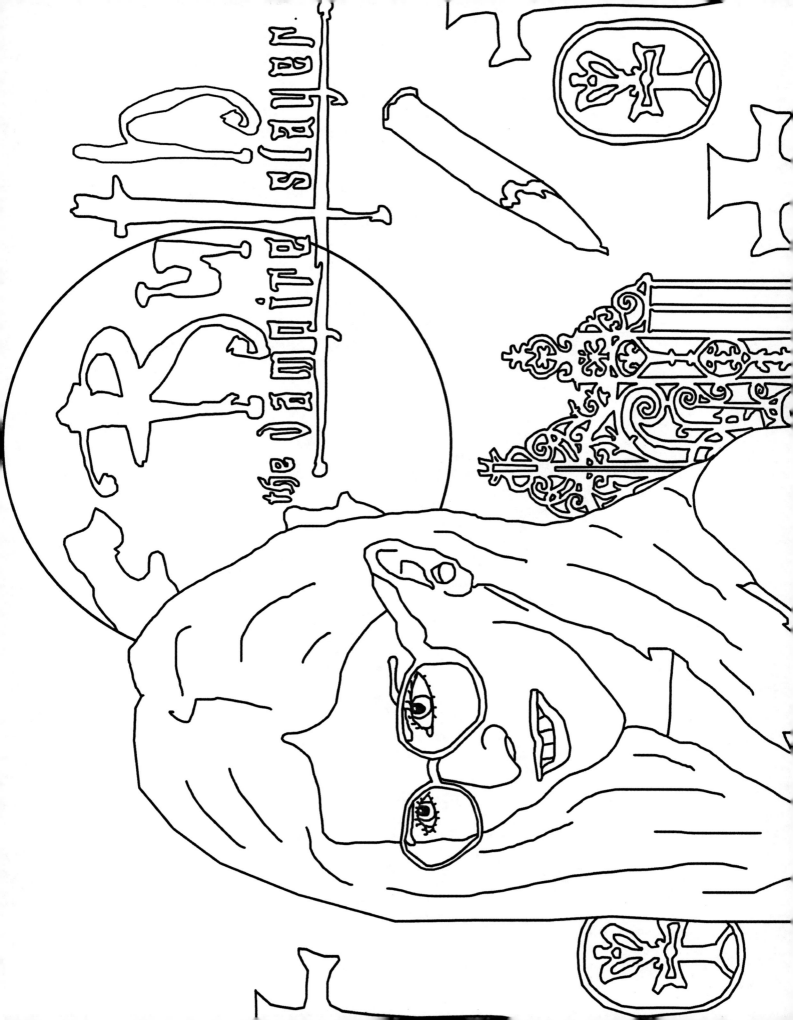

RBG's love affair with her husband Marty Ginsburg lasted for more than a half-century. Shortly before his death in 2010, Marty wrote, "I have admired and loved you almost since the day we first met at Cornell some 56 years ago."

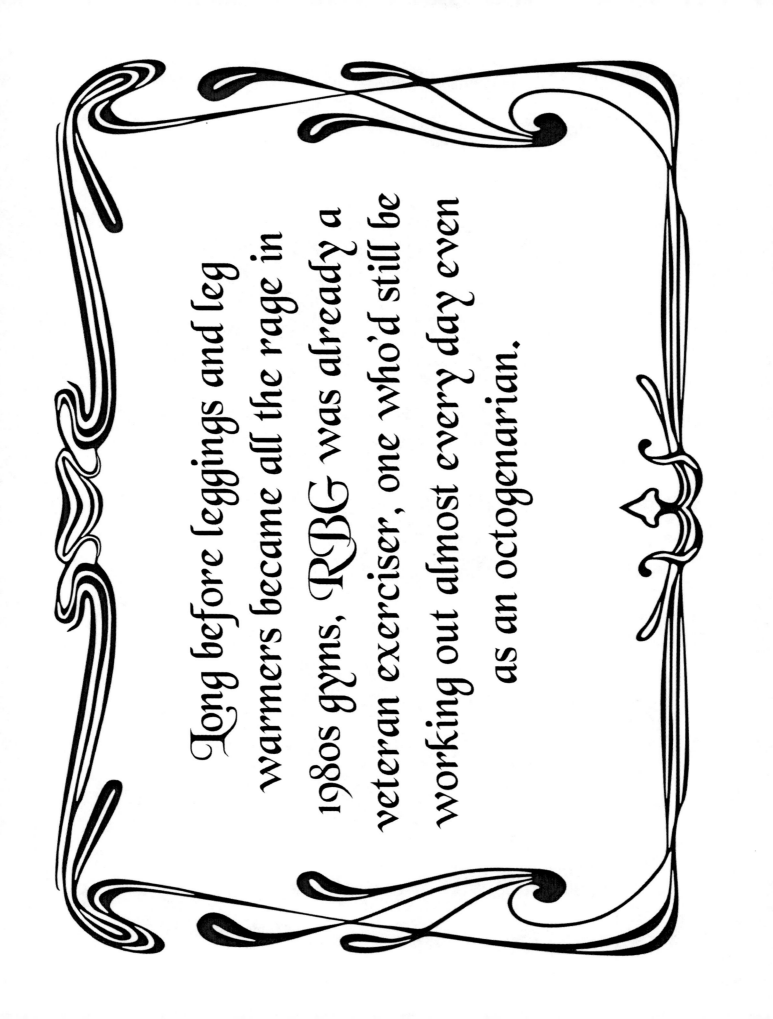

Long before leggings and leg warmers became all the rage in 1980s gyms, RBG was already a veteran exerciser, one who'd still be working out almost every day even as an octogenarian.

If RBG had been cast as a Charlie's Angel in the late 1970s, she would have played Sabrina.

Despite her small stature, RBG has long been an avid outdoorsperson, riding horses, paddle boarding, waterskiing, and even whitewater rafting.

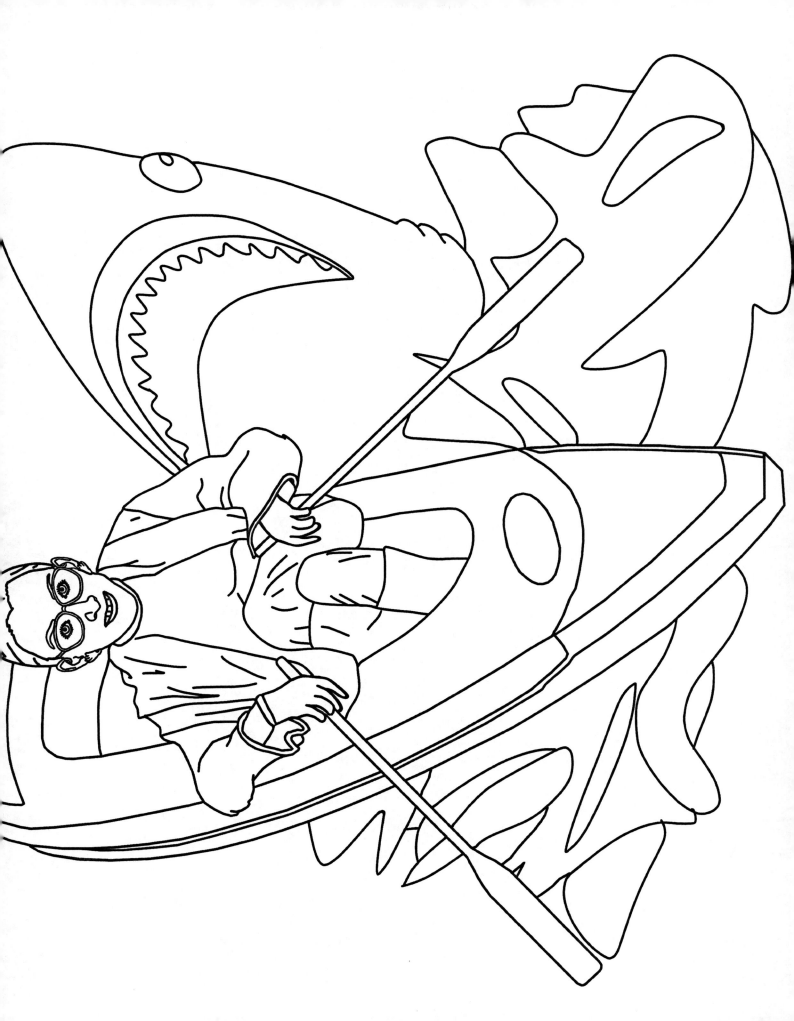

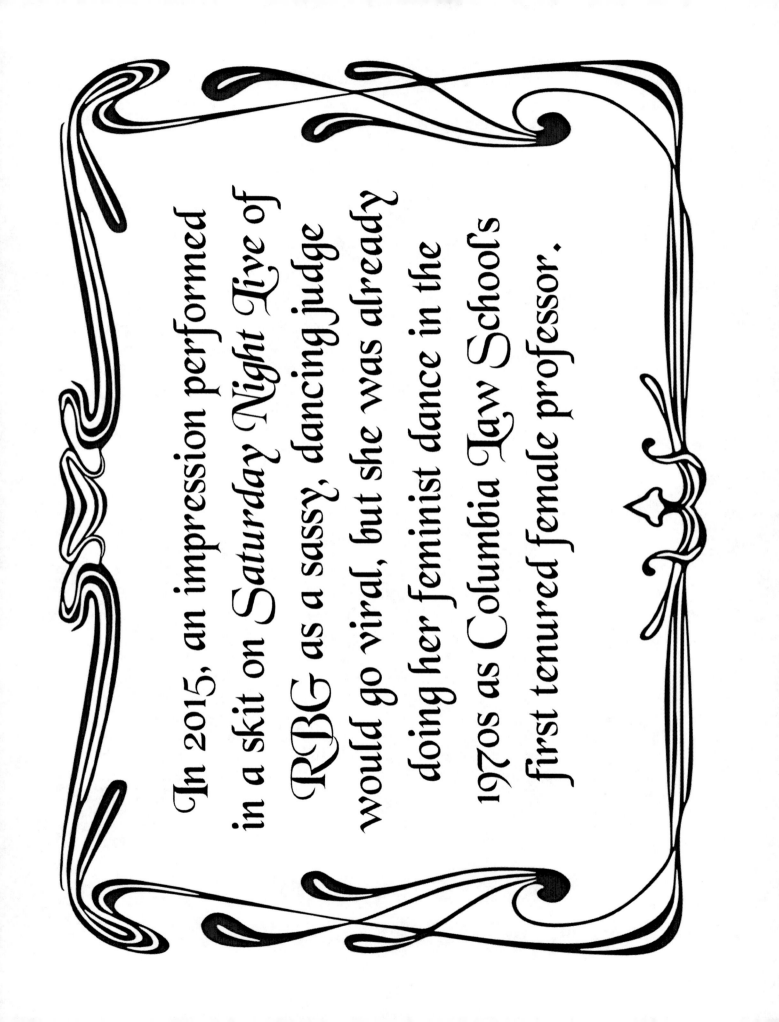

In 2015, an impression performed in a skit on *Saturday Night Live* of RBG as a sassy, dancing judge would go viral, but she was already doing her feminist dance in the 1970s as Columbia Law School's first tenured female professor.

RBG is such a bad cook that her husband Marty taught himself the culinary arts early on in their marriage and eventually became the sole chef for the family.

Although RBG was never a real hippie, her championing of women's reproductive rights in the 1960s and 70s still cast her as a maverick during this period of rapid national change.

RBG admits to being a terrible driver, having failed her driving test five times as a young woman. But she wasn't afraid to take to the open road in the 1950s, enrolling first in Cornell and then in Harvard Law School.

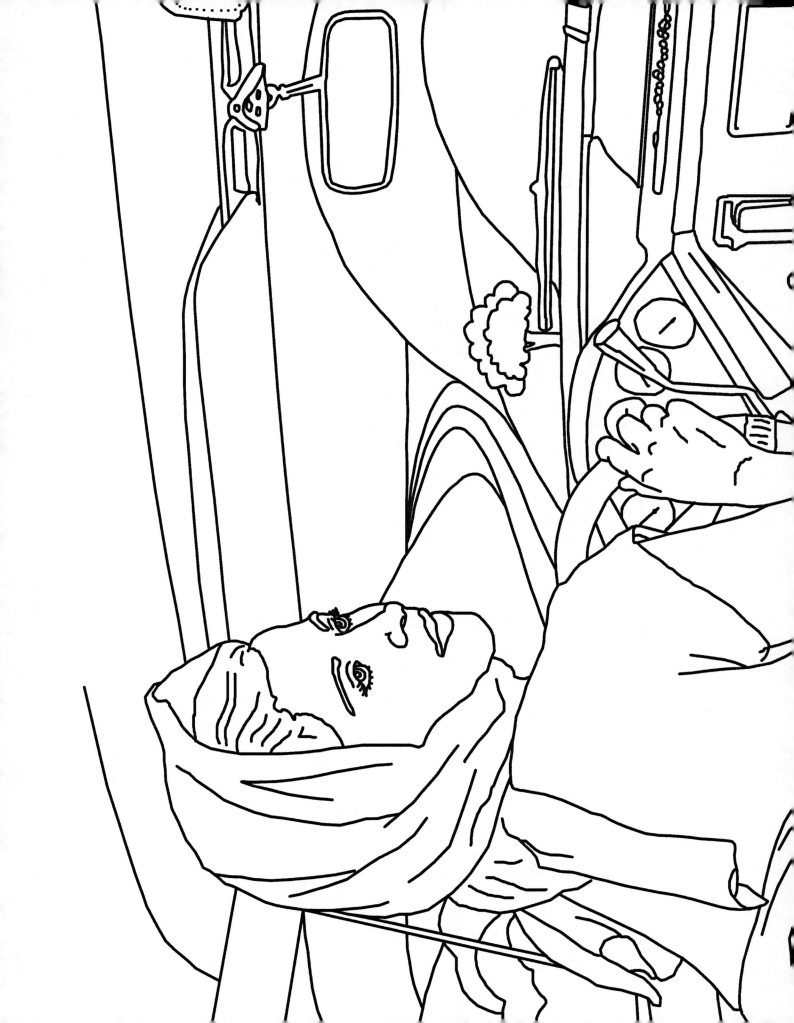

When Rosie the Riveter appeared on posters during World War II, RBG was a cherub-faced girl, not even ten years old. But her later championing of equal rights for women would make her as important a feminist symbol as Rosie, in whose footsteps she followed.

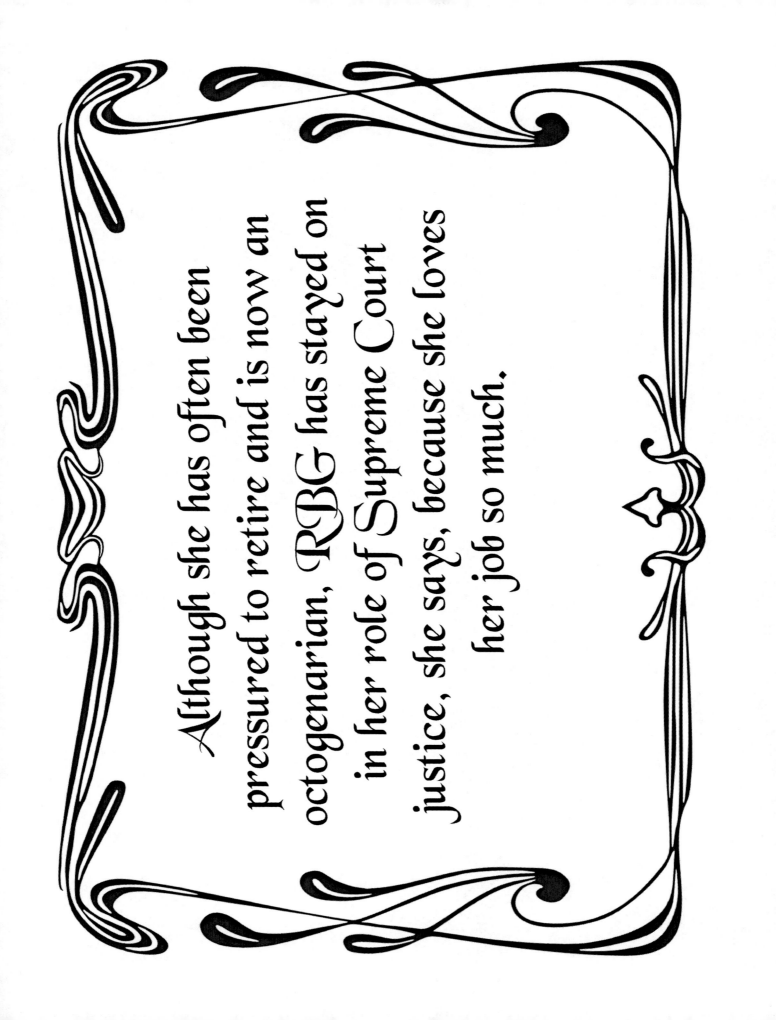

Although she has often been pressured to retire and is now an octogenarian, RBG has stayed on in her role of Supreme Court justice, she says, because she loves her job so much.